OSPREY MILITARY

MEN-AT-A

WELLINGTON'S GENERALS

Text by
MICHAEL BARTHORP
Colour plates by
RICHARD HOOK

First published in Great Britain in 1978 by
Osprey, an imprint of Reed Consumer Books Limited
Michelin House, 81 Fulham Road, London SW3 6RB
© Copyright 1978 Reed International Books Limited
Reprinted 1990, 1994

ISBN 0 85045 299 6

Filmset by BAS Printers Limited,
Over Wallop, Hampshire
Printed in Hong Kong

The Command and Staff System of Wellington's Army

Up to the outbreak of the Napoleonic Wars the most usual, though not the only, method of obtaining a commission in the British army was by purchase. Thereafter, further promotion was either by purchase of the next step in rank, by seniority without purchase, or by the patronage of the commander-in-chief. This applied up to and including the rank of lieutenant-colonel. Above that rank, promotion was entirely by seniority, the date on which an officer achieved his lieutenant-colonelcy determining his seniority for life. In theory any lieutenant-colonel could expect, in due course of time, to attain the rank of general, quite regardless of whether he was ever employed in any of the intervening ranks; he only had to live long enough. In 1811 three major-generals were promoted lieutenant-general, none of whom had seen any service since the American Revolution! The officer would only receive pay for the higher ranks, however, if he was actually employed as a colonel or a general officer, and then only for the duration of that employment. Once he ceased to be so employed, his pay reverted to that of his regimental rank.

Ludicrous though the system sounds, it had advantages in that there was no limit to the number of generals in the army, and there was no obligation

Wellington and generals at the Battle of Nivelle, 1813. Above his right hand is Beresford, on his left is Cotton, above whose left shoulder are Colville, Dalhousie and Picton. Cole and Hill are looking towards the pointing hussar officer on the right. After Heaphy. (National Army Museum)

to employ those who had reached that rank. Thus, if it was desired to promote a promising younger officer, all that was required was to raise all those senior to him to the next higher rank, however aged or useless they may have been. In 1813, eighty-one colonels were promoted major-general in order that the 82nd in seniority could be appointed to a major-general's command in the field, and, in 1814, ninety-one lieutenant-generals and major-generals were promoted to the next higher rank, so that Major-General Charles Stewart could be advanced to lieutenant-general. The only exception to this ponderous system was the promotion, in 1813, of Wellington himself to field-marshal, when, at the age of forty-four, he jumped ahead of some one hundred and forty officers senior to him to a rank in which none of the previous incumbents, other than Royal dukes, had been less than sixty-one years old on appointment.

Front and rear of the embroidered coat of a lieutenant-general. Note the buttons in threes. (National Army Museum)

Sir John Hope (1765–1823), 3rd Earl of Hopetoun, in the undress uniform of a lieutenant-general, c. 1814. Adjutant-General to Abercromby in Egypt, 1801; brigade commander in the Hanover expedition, 1805; lieutenant-general in Moore's Corunna campaign, 1808–09; divisional commander at Walcheren, 1809; commanded the 1st Division of the Peninsular army in 1813 and the left wing of the army in 1814. After Raeburn. (National Army Museum)

The system resulted in a serious dearth of senior officers who were both young and competent enough to take command of Wellington's brigades and divisions in the field. The provision of officers for these appointments was the responsibility of the Military Secretary at the Horse Guards in London, and, as a general rule, Wellington, as commander in the field, had to make do with what he was sent. While the Military Secretary, Colonel Torrens, did his best to select suitable officers, Wellington also found himself saddled with the likes of the short-sighted and drunken Sir William Erskine. When Wellington remonstrated against Erskine's appointment on the grounds that he was 'generally understood to be a madman', Torrens replied: 'No doubt he is sometimes a little mad, but in his lucid

Staff officers, c. 1813. Adjutant-General or Quartermaster-General (mounted) and Assistant AG or QMG. Soldiers of the Royal Staff Corps in the background. After Hamilton Smith. (National Army Museum)

intervals he is an uncommonly clever fellow; and I trust he will have no fit during the campaign, though he looked a little wild as he embarked'. It is small wonder that Wellington felt constrained to write: 'Really when I reflect upon the character and attainments of some of the General officers of this army, I tremble'.

Wellington had little say in the appointment of general officers, and of the eighty-five officers who served in the field as commanders or on the staff, in the rank of major-general and above between 1809 and 1815, only Beresford, Hill, Picton, Craufurd, Graham, Houston, Leith and Nightingall were men whom he had particularly requested. All these, with the exception of Nightingall, turned out successfully, within their own limitations. However, it was these limitations, particularly when commanding formations larger than a brigade, that caused Wellington most concern. Almost all were brave, but what was most lacking was 'a cool, discriminating judgement in action' and the ability 'to convey their orders, and act with vigour and decision, that the soldiers will look up to them with confidence, in the moment of action, and obey

them with alacrity'. The lack of these qualities, even among his better commanders, caused him to write: 'They are really heroes when I am on the spot to direct them, but when I am obliged to quit them they are children.'

With the exception of Graham, who as will be seen did not join the army until he was forty-five, Wellington's senior officers were all, good or bad, comparatively young. On average they had received their ensign's commissions at the age of seventeen, reaching lieutenant-colonel at around twenty-eight, and major-general at forty. One of the most senior and most competent, Edward Paget, had been a lieutenant-colonel at eighteen and a major-general at thirty. This does not include general officers of the Royal Artillery and Royal Engineers, whose promotion from first commissioning was entirely by seniority and consequently much slower.

Of the eighty-five general officers who served Wellington, three were peers in their own right while twenty-one were the sons of peers or baronets. The remainder had either legal, clerical or service backgrounds or came from the country gentry. Twenty-two had been to public schools but most had been educated privately and only seven had attended university. A mere twelve had received any military education before joining the army, either at the Royal Military College or continental military academies. This, however, was balanced by the practical experience gained by many on active service since 1793 in the Low Countries, the West Indies, India, the Mediterranean and Egypt.

Whatever their failings as commanders or senior staff officers, lack of courage was not among them. Casualties from death, wounds, or being taken prisoner were quite common among formation commanders, and indeed this readiness to lead from the front, and show unconcern in the face of danger, could on occasion prove detrimental to the proper performance of their duties. The incompetent Skerrett, briefly and disastrously in command of the Light Division, was observed by an officer, 'standing in the most exposed spot under the enemy's fire as stupidly composed for himself as inactive for the welfare of his command'. Only in three cases was the courage of Wellington's generals suspect: Long, whose poor showing may have been more inspired by his revulsion with war than want of bravery; Slade, like Long a cavalry commander; and Hay, of whom it was said: 'That he is a paltry, plundering old wretch is established beyond doubt. That he is no officer is as clear, and that he wants spirit is firmly believed'.

The formations entrusted to these general officers were initially, for Wellington's Oporto operations in 1809, eight British and one King's German Legion infantry brigades, each being a major-general's command, and comprising between two and four battalions, a company of the 5th (Rifle) Battalion 60th Foot and, in five brigades, a Portuguese battalion. The cavalry was formed in a division of two brigades. The Talavera campaign of the same year saw the first divisional organization of the infantry. The 1st Division had four brigades, one Guards, one Line and two K.G.L., each of two battalions, while the 2nd, 3rd and 4th had two brigades, each of two or three battalions. Wellington envisaged the divisions being commanded by lieutenant-generals, but as he only had two, the senior major-general of brigade was to take temporary command.

Early in 1810 Wellington began attaching Portuguese brigades, each of one *Caçador* (rifle) and two Line battalions, to his existing British divisions, and at the same time created the Light Division, formed of Craufurd's Light Brigade (43rd, 52nd and 95th) and two Portuguese *Caçador* battalions. He visualized this formation providing the same service for the army as a whole, as the rifle companies of the 5th/60th performed for the brigades. In August 1810 the 5th Division was formed and, in the winter of 1810–11, with the arrival of fresh battalions from home, he was able to form the 6th and 7th Divisions. Thereafter no new divisions were formed, and from 1811 the infantry organization remained largely as follows: the Light Division as before but with the addition of two, later three, battalions; the 1st Division with two British and one K.G.L. brigades; the 2nd with three British brigades and Hamilton's Portuguese division attached to it, forming a small corps; and the remainder, 3rd–7th, having two British and one Portuguese brigades. A British brigade usually had three battalions and a company of riflemen, a Portuguese five battalions and a company of *caçadores*. To make each division self-contained with its own artillery, one field battery, either British or Portuguese, was attached from 1811, increasing to two batteries in 1812. A horse artillery battery was attached to the Light Division.

Apart from the Light Division, which had the 1st K.G.L. Hussars almost permanently attached, the infantry divisions had no cavalry. This remained organized in one division of three, later seven, brigades, each of two regiments, except for a period between 1811 and 1813 when it was split into two divisions, one of four brigades, the other of two. However, the cavalry was seldom used in mass under its own commander, Cotton, but was deployed by brigades under the direct orders of Wellington.

Up to Vittoria in 1813, Wellington exercised direct control over his divisional commanders with no intermediate level of command, except for the force in Estramadura, the 2nd Division, Hamilton's Portuguese and two cavalry brigades, which formed a more or less independent corps under Hill. This direct control stemmed largely from Wellington having no senior officer of sufficient ability, other than Hill, whom he felt he could

Sabretache of general officer of hussars worn by Lord Uxbridge at Waterloo. (National Army Museum)

entrust with the command of a corps of two or more divisions. The officers appointed as his second-in-command between 1809 and 1813, Sherbrooke and then Brent Spencer, who in theory should have been able to undertake such a task, were quite unfitted for it. Spencer was 'exceedingly puzzle-headed' and always referred to the Tagus as the Thames. He was replaced in 1813 by Graham, an admirable officer in many ways, but lacking experience with a large command and suffering from increasing blindness.

After Vittoria, owing to the difficulty of exercising personal command over eight divisions in the broken country and wide frontages of the Pyrenees, Wellington organized the army into three almost permanent corps, or rather a centre and two wings: the left under Graham, until ill-health forced him to return home, when he was replaced by the able Hope, the right under Hill, while the centre, as strong as the two wings combined, Wellington kept under his direct control, with Beresford acting as his second-in-command and occasionally commanding half of it.

In the Waterloo campaign the Allied army was organized thus: two corps, commanded respectively by the Prince of Orange and Hill, the former having four infantry and one Dutch cavalry divisions, the latter three divisions; a reserve of two British divisions and two Allied contingents under Wellington's direct control; and the Anglo-German cavalry of eight brigades under Uxbridge. Apart from the 1st (Guards) Division, the British divisions consisted of two British or K.G.L. brigades and one Hanoverian brigade, although the 6th Division had only one of each; each division had two field batteries. The British brigades had between two and four battalions, the Hanoverian between four and six. The cavalry brigades had, on average, three regiments. At Waterloo itself, the corps organization was not really of much consequence, since Wellington exercised complete control over the whole army, at times giving orders direct to brigades and even to battalions.

To assist commanders at each level in the execution of their duties were the members of the staff. These fell into three categories: personal staff; the officers of the Adjutant-General's and Quartermaster-General's Departments; and the staff of the civil departments—Commissary-General's, Paymaster-General's and Medical. The first category included aides-de-camp and brigade-majors. The former were all young men, chosen by the general they served to perform such duties as writing letters, carrying messages and organizing the general's personal establishment. In an age when all orders had to be passed by word of mouth or in writing, the ADC was a vital link in the chain of command. Brigade-majors were concerned with the daily routine of their brigades and implementing the orders of the brigade commander, who had no other military staff officer, unless he was entitled to an ADC. Lieutenant-generals were allowed two ADCs and Wellington himself seldom had less than six. The Adjutant-General's and Quartermaster-General's Departments provided the channels through which commanders, above brigade level, issued their orders, and arranged for the daily management of the formation they served. Under Wellington, due to the proven reliability of George Murray, who served as Quartermaster-General throughout the Peninsular War with only one break, that department became pre-eminent, while the Adjutant-General's remained largely concerned with routine matters such as discipline, strength returns, supervision of clothing and armaments and the issue of regulations. The Quartermaster-General's work was involved with the conduct of operations and posed problems that changed daily—the quartering and movement of the army, allocation of transport, acquisition of intelligence about the countryside and the enemy, and the maintenance of communications.

At Wellington's own headquarters, apart from his personal staff of ADCs and his Military Secretary, who was responsible, *inter alia*, for his financial business and all matters regarding officers' appointments, there would be the Adjutant-General, with perhaps two Assistant AGs (lieutenant-colonels or majors) and two Deputy Assistant AGs (captains or subalterns), and the Quartermaster-General with a similar staff, both departments having their own quota of clerks, orderlies and servants. At a divisional headquarters there might be only one Assistant AG and an Assistant QMG with a deputy.

The civil departments would all be represented at the main headquarters, and in the case of the Commissary-General's, responsible for the procuring, storing and issuing of all manner of stores and

Sir Thomas Graham, Baron Lynedoch of Balgowan, in the
embroidered uniform of a lieutenant-general, c. 1814. After
Lawrence. (National Army Museum)

Henry Paget, Earl of Uxbridge, later Marquess of Anglesey, in the uniform of colonel of the 7th Hussars. (National Army Museum)

supplies, there would be officials at both divisional and brigade level.

Apart from these three categories of staff, there were also to be found at Wellington's headquarters his Commanders Royal Artillery and Royal Engineers with their staffs, the Provost-Marshal and his assistants, also represented at divisional headquarters, and the Deputy-Judge-Advocate-General.

Henry Paget, Earl of Uxbridge

Henry Paget was born on 17 May 1768, the eldest son of the Earl of Uxbridge. After being educated at Westminster and Christ Church, Oxford, he served briefly in the regiment of Staffordshire Militia commanded by his father. The outbreak of war with revolutionary France in 1793 required the expansion of the army, so Paget raised the 80th Foot, chiefly from among his father's tenantry, and

at the age of twenty-five, with no proper military experience, was granted the temporary rank of lieutenant-colonel in command of the 80th. He took his regiment to join the Duke of York's army for the unfortunate campaign in Flanders in 1794 and soon found himself commanding a brigade. His real wish, however, was to transfer to the cavalry: 'I own I am disgusted with the Infantry and the 80th and think Cavalry so infinitely preferable.' Eventually, through lobbying his father, he obtained a permanent lieutenant-colonelcy in the 16th Light Dragoons, after receiving regular commissions for all the lower ranks over a space of three months. On 6 April 1797 he obtained command of the 7th Light Dragoons and over the next four years made it one of the finest regiments in the army. He distinguished himself in the disastrous 1799 campaign in Holland, where, in command of a brigade consisting of the 7th and 15th Light Dragoons, he routed a superior force of French cavalry. In 1802 he was promoted major-general and in 1808, after only fifteen years' service, lieutenant-general.

Later that year he was given command of the cavalry division in Sir John Moore's army in Portugal, joining Moore in late November after the latter had advanced to Salamanca to threaten the French lines of communication. When the advance continued, Paget was sent ahead towards Sahagun with the 10th and 15th Hussars. Arriving there before daylight he found it occupied by the French, so, leaving the 10th to advance upon the town, he led the 15th round to its rear to cut off the enemy's retreat. However, the alarm was given and Paget found himself confronted by 600 dragoons. Though the 15th only mustered 400 sabres and the 10th had not yet come up, Paget immediately charged, routing the dragoons and taking 167 prisoners. Moore called the action 'a handsome thing and well done'. Two days later Moore learned that Napoleon himself was advancing upon him from Madrid so, rather than risk the loss of the only army England had in the field, he ordered a retreat. During the terrible retreat to Corunna Paget earned high praise for his handling of the cavalry, which kept the French horse from the heels of the infantry, particularly with a dashing charge at Benavente on 29 December.

Paget was not to serve in the Peninsula again, for, shortly after his return from Corunna, he chose to desert his wife and elope with Lady Charlotte Wellesley, Wellington's sister-in-law. With Wellington now in command in Portugal, there was no place for Paget in his army. Though given an infantry division in the Walcheren Expedition, his undoubted talents as a cavalry leader were wasted until 1815.

He succeeded his father in 1812 and on 2 January 1815 was made G.C.B. In the spring he was appointed to command all the cavalry and horse artillery of the army Wellington was then assembling in Flanders, following Napoleon's return from Elba. On 17 June he covered, with his cavalry, the withdrawal from Quatre Bras to Waterloo, bringing the French advance guard to a halt at Genappe by his handling of his own regiment, the 7th, now hussars, and two squadrons of the 1st Life Guards, supported by horse artillery.

At Waterloo he ordered the Union Brigade to charge D'Erlon's corps when it attacked the British left. He himself led forward the Household Cavalry against Milhaud's cuirassiers, but was unable to prevent them or the Union Brigade from charging too far. He went back to bring forward his second line to cover the retirement of the heavy cavalry, but it was too far to the rear and the heavies, though successful in their charge, suffered severe casualties. In the closing stages of the battle he was wounded in the knee and his leg had to be amputated.

On 4 July 1815 he was created Marquess of Anglesey and in 1818 was made a Knight of the Garter. In later life he served as Master-General of the Ordnance and proved a very popular Lord-Lieutenant of Ireland. He was promoted field-marshal in 1846 and died in 1854, aged eighty-six.

Thomas Graham

Graham was unique among Wellington's commanders in that he did not begin his military career until middle age. He was born on 19 October 1748, the third son of Thomas Graham, Laird of Balgowan in Perthshire, and was educated privately and at Christ Church, Oxford. In 1774 he married Lord Cathcart's beautiful daughter, Mary, who was subsequently painted four times by Gainsborough. The couple lived abroad for some years on account of Mrs Graham's poor health, but on returning home he purchased an estate in Perthshire to which, being a keen agriculturalist and sportsman, he devoted close attention. In 1790 they again went abroad, but Mrs Graham died in southern France in 1792. When Graham was bringing her body home for burial, the coffin was opened at Toulouse by revolutionary officials in search of contraband. Appalled by this incident, Graham decided to devote his life to fighting the excesses of the French Revolution.

In July 1793 he got himself attached as unofficial ADC to Lord Mulgrave during the operations at Toulon, and on his return home he raised, at his own expense, the 90th Foot. For this he was granted a temporary lieutenant-colonelcy on 10 February 1794. He served with his regiment during the Quiberon Bay expedition and in 1796 was appointed British Military Commissioner to the Austrian Army in Italy. Besieged with Wurmser in Mantua, he escaped in a snowstorm, taking news of the garrison's plight to the Austrian headquarters. From 1798 he served in the Mediterranean until the Peace of Amiens. He accompanied Moore to Sweden in 1808 and to Spain, where he was present

Lieutenant-General of Cavalry, c. 1812. The hat bore a gilt star loop, not visible in the illustration. After Hamilton Smith. (National Army Museum)

at the latter's death at Corunna. Though he had tried for some years to have his military rank made permanent, it was only as a result of Moore's dying request that this was granted, with seniority from the date of his temporary lieutenant-colonelcy in 1794.

Now aged fifty, he was officially promoted major-general and commanded a brigade at Walcheren, but had to be invalided home. In 1810 he was sent to command the garrison at Cadiz with the rank of lieutenant-general. From here, in February 1811, he launched an attack against the rear of the French force blockading him, and a month later won a victory at Barrosa. In June he joined Wellington's main army and was given the 1st Division. To this command were added the 6th and 7th Divisions, thus forming a corps, with which he provided part of the covering force for the final siege and capture of Badajoz the following January. During the advance to Salamanca he commanded the same force with two brigades of cavalry added, but an eye infection forced his return to England twelve days before the battle of 22 July.

He was back in the Peninsula by early 1813 in time for the Vittoria campaign. Wellington sent Graham with a corps of 20,000, including the 1st and 5th Divisions, two Portuguese brigades and a Spanish force, on a wide sweep round the French army at Vittoria to cut the main road to France in their rear. This manoeuvre, which was to prove fatal to French morale, was completely successful and, after blocking the road, Graham attacked the French from the rear as Wellington broke through the centre. Only the mass of plunder left by the French, which distracted Wellington's troops from pursuit, enabled the remains of King Joseph's army to escape by side roads.

After Vittoria Graham was sent on after the French rearguards towards St Sebastian, round which he threw a blockade on 28 June. While the rest of the army engaged Soult in the Pyrenees, Graham besieged St Sebastian with the 5th Division and a Portuguese brigade, but it was not until September, when Wellington was able to release further troops after defeating Soult, that the town fell. The success of the final assault was largely due to Graham's bold decision, unusual at that time, to order his artillery to fire over the heads of the attacking infantry. Graham commanded the left wing at the crossing of the Bidassoa, but his recurring eye trouble and failing health compelled him to hand over to Sir John Hope.

He took the field again in November when he was sent with a force to capture Antwerp in conjunction with the Prussians, but his failure to take Bergen-op-Zoom in February 1814 was an unhappy end to an otherwise distinguished military career.

Graham was greatly respected by all ranks and his popularity rivalled Hill's in the Peninsular army. He had been made a Knight of the Bath in March 1812, and in May 1814 was created Baron Lynedoch of Balgowan, subsequently receiving the G.C.B. and G.C.M.G. In later life he founded the United Services Club as a meeting place for officers and devoted himself to agriculture, sport and politics, until he died at the great age of ninety-five on 18 December 1843.

Edward Paget

A younger brother of Henry Paget, Edward was born on 3 November 1775 and educated at Westminster. Receiving a cornetcy in the Life Guards in March 1792, nine months later he was a captain in the 54th Foot and by April 1794, at the age of only eighteen, he was lieutenant-colonel commanding the 28th Foot. Despite his youth, he had a flair for command and led his regiment with great confidence in the Flanders campaign of 1794–95. His elder brother wrote of him: 'I am told he has a very fine Regiment and is everything he ought to be'. In 1797 he was at the Battle of Cape St Vincent and the following year was made a colonel in the army and an ADC to the King. He fought throughout the Egyptian campaign of 1801, being wounded at the Battle of Alexandria, where the 28th particularly distinguished themselves under his leadership. In October 1803 he was made a brigadier-general and, on 1 January 1805, a major-general.

From 1806 he served in the Mediterranean and in January 1808 went with Moore's expedition to Sweden in command of the Reserve, the picked troops of the army. Later that year he was in the

The capture of Sir Edward Paget by French cavalry, 1812, when he was a lieutenant-general and second-in-command to Wellington. After Atkinson. (National Army Museum)

Corunna campaign, commanding the rearguard with great skill during the retreat. At the Battle of Corunna his handling of his brigade was responsible for the defeat of Soult's flank attack against the British right. He was a handsome man with a commanding presence and Blakeney of the 28th said that when Paget 'gave an order, there was something peculiar in his glance, impressive in his tone of voice, and decisive in his manner. The order was clear. The execution must be prompt'.

Under Wellington he was promoted local lieutenant-general and commanded the left wing of the army during the advance from Coimbra to Oporto in 1809. He led the attack across the Douro above Oporto on 12 May, and held the seminary against French counter-attacks with only 600 men while the main force crossed, being wounded in the arm, which had to be amputated.

He had to return to England to recover from this wound, thus missing the campaigns of 1810–11. He was made lieutenant-general in the army on 4 June 1811, now aged thirty-five, and received the K.B. on 12 June 1812. In the autumn of that year he

returned to the Peninsula as Wellington's second-in-command, but, during the retreat of the army from Burgos, while trying to close a gap between the 5th and 7th Divisions, he was surprised by three French cavalrymen on 17 November. Being unable to defend himself with only one arm and escorted by a single Spanish orderly, he was taken prisoner. His capture lost to the army a brave and talented commander, whose only defect was short-sightedness, which Wellington believed 'was the immediate cause of his being taken'.

In January 1815 he was made G.C.B. but took no part in the Waterloo campaign. In 1822 he went out to India as Commander-in-Chief and was responsible for the operations of the Burma War of 1824–25. In 1825 he was promoted general and subsequently became Governor of Chelsea Hospital, a post he held until his death on 13 May 1849. With his brilliant early career and his undoubted competence, Edward Paget should have become

Sir Stapleton Cotton, later Viscount Combermere, in the uniform of a general officer of hussars. After Heaphy. (National Portrait Gallery)

one of Wellington's most distinguished commanders, but the wound he received at Oporto and his capture prevented him from achieving the fame which otherwise should have attended him.

Stapleton Cotton

Born on 14 November 1773, the second son of Sir Robert Cotton, Bt., Stapleton Cotton was educated at Westminster and a military academy in London, receiving his first commission in the 23rd Royal Welch Fusiliers in 1790. He transferred to the cavalry, in which he was to make his name, as captain in the 6th Dragoons in 1793, serving in the Flanders campaign of 1793–94. At the age of twenty he obtained the lieutenant-colonelcy of the 25th Light Dragoons, which he commanded at the Cape and in the Seringapatam campaign in India in 1799, where he first met Wellington. Transferring to the 16th Light Dragoons in 1800, he was promoted colonel the same year and major-general five years later. In 1808 he commanded a brigade of the 14th and 16th Light Dragoons on the Portuguese frontier during the Corunna campaign and

later at Oporto and Talavera.

Having become his father's heir on the death of his elder brother in 1800, he succeeded to the title in January 1810 and had to go home on family business. Despite these new responsibilities, he chose to return to the Peninsula and, as a local lieutenant-general, was given command of all Wellington's cavalry. In this capacity he covered the retreat to the Lines of Torres Vedras without, it is said, losing a single baggage wagon.

Until 1813 Wellington was always weak in cavalry and those regiments he had were seldom used in mass, as was the French practice, so purely cavalry encounters were few. However, in April 1812, Cotton, having been promoted lieutenant-general in the army in January, fought a well-organized little battle at Llerena with two brigades against Soult's rearguard cavalry, forcing the French marshal to withdraw. Just before Salamanca he was in command of Wellington's rearguard, and his handling of this force, consisting of the 14th Light Dragoons and the 4th and Light Divisions, in the face of Marmont's army which had suddenly changed direction on 18 July, enabled Wellington to regroup his forces successfully. At Salamanca itself the decisive cavalry charge against Maucune's division, led by Le Marchant's heavy brigade, inspired Wellington to exclaim: 'By God, Cotton, I never saw anything so beautiful in my life; the day is *yours*'.

Cotton was wounded in the right arm by a shot from a Portuguese picquet after Salamanca and had to go home, where he was awarded the Order of the Bath. He returned to the army in 1813 three days after Vittoria and commanded the cavalry all through the closing stages of the Peninsular War.

Cotton was an excellent horseman and was noted for the magnificent appearance of his uniform and horse furniture, which was reputed to be worth 500 guineas. He was brave, and was known as the 'Lion d'Or'. Despite his own love of finery, he had a keen eye for serviceability rather than mere smartness among his cavalrymen, and he never tired men or

Rowland Hill

Sir Rowland Hill, later Viscount Hill, in the undress uniform of a lieutenant-general, 1819. After Dawe. (National Army Museum)

horses unnecessarily. His ability as a cavalry commander has been accorded mixed judgements, but Wellington thought 'he commands our cavalry very well'.

In 1814 he was raised to the peerage as Baron Combermere. Although Wellington hoped to have him commanding the cavalry for the Waterloo campaign, the post went to Uxbridge, but Cotton joined the army in Paris, where he commanded the cavalry of the army of occupation.

After serving consecutively as Governor of Barbados and Commander-in-Chief in Ireland, he was appointed to the chief command in India from 1825–30, where he led the successful operations against the Jats, culminating in the taking of the great fortress of Bhurtpore. He became a viscount in 1827 and a field-marshal in 1855. He spent the last thirty years of his life attending to his estates and parliamentary duties until he died on 21 February 1865, aged ninety-one.

Of all Wellington's senior officers, Hill was not only the most dependable, he was also the most popular with all ranks. Born on 11 August 1772, the second son of a Shropshire gentleman, he joined the army in 1790 as an ensign in the 38th Foot, transferring to the 53rd a year later but spending two years at the military school in Strasbourg. In 1793 he earned 'golden opinions' while serving as an ADC at the siege of Toulon, where he was noticed by Graham, who had him appointed to a majority in the latter's new regiment, the 90th. In May 1794 he became lieutenant-colonel in the 90th, which he made into a fine regiment, and commanded it during the Egyptian campaign of 1801. By 1805 he was a major-general commanding a brigade in the Hanover expedition, and three years later he was present at the first British victories in the Peninsula, Rolica and Vimiero. He led a brigade in the Corunna campaign and also, after returning to Portugal, during the Oporto operations of 1809. Later that year he was given the 2nd Division, with which he held the important Cerro de Medellin feature at Talavera.

During 1810 Wellington entrusted him with the independent command of a small corps in defence of the Portuguese frontier between the Rivers Gaudiana and Tagus. This, in view of Wellington's preference for keeping a tight control over his subordinates, shows the faith the commander had in Hill's reliability. In the winter he had to go home with malaria, handing over his command to Beresford, under whom it suffered heavily at Albuera. Hill returned in May and was ordered to take command of the force in Estramadura, 10,000 strong including the 2nd and 4th Divisions, watching Wellington's right flank as he besieged Badajoz. After the main army began the blockade of Ciudad Rodrigo in August, Hill made a masterly surprise attack at Arroyo dos Molinos, completely routing the force opposing him and taking 1,300 prisoners for the loss of only 7 killed and 64 wounded.

On 1 January 1812 he was promoted lieutenant-general and two months later was admitted to the Order of the Bath. His corps and Graham's formed the covering force in southern and eastern Estramadura while Wellington began the final siege of Badajoz, and in May he conducted another fine operation which resulted in the destruction of the French forts and bridge at Almaraz. When the Salamanca campaign began, Hill was again left to protect the rear of the main army against any attack from Soult in Andalusia and later, when Wellington was at Burgos, he carried out the same protective role against three French armies.

Throughout the final campaigns of 1813–14 Hill commanded a corps the strength of which varied, but which included British, Spanish and Portuguese divisions with, as its permanent backbone, his old 2nd Division. He began the attack on the right at Vittoria; he prevented any relief of, or break out from, Pamplona during Soult's counter-offensive at Sorauren; and of St Pierre, near Bayonne, where he was attacked by Soult with a force twice his strength, Wellington said that he, Hill, had given the French 'the soundest thrashing they had ever had'. St Pierre was said to be only the second occasion when Hill had been heard to swear! Intelligent, energetic, ever thoughtful and considerate for the needs of his men, he was above all entirely trustworthy, and Wellington always knew that any task given to Hill would be planned and carried out with care, foresight and drive. No man, be he exhausted British private, wounded French prisoner, or dispossessed Spanish peasant, was beneath Hill's charitable attentions, and it is little wonder that he was known affectionately by his troops as 'Daddy Hill'.

After the Peninsular War he was created Baron Hill of Almaraz and Hardwicke. As soon as news of Napoleon's escape from Elba reached London, he was sent to Brussels to supervise the preparations made for war by the young Prince of Orange. For the Waterloo campaign he was given a corps consisting of the 2nd and 4th Divisions and various allied formations. In the closing stages of the battle he rode to the head of Adam's brigade (52nd, 71st and 95th) to lead the counter-attack on the Imperial Guard. His horse was shot and, seeing him fall, his staff thought he had been killed, but found that he was only severely concussed.

Hill accompanied the army to Paris and served as second-in-command of the army of occupation until 1818. Thereafter he retired to his estate in Shropshire and, refusing all important offices

Sir Edward Barnes (1776–1838). Staff officer in the Peninsula, 1812. Major-General, 1813. Commanded a brigade at Vittoria, Pyrenees, Nivelle, Nive and Orthes. Appointed Adjutant-General for the Waterloo campaign and severely wounded on 18 June 1815. After Heaphy. (National Portrait Gallery)

offered to him, devoted himself to the pursuits of the country gentleman, the best type of which he so clearly typified. When Wellington became Prime Minister in 1828, he accepted the post of Commander-in-Chief of the Army, which he held for fourteen years. He was made a general in 1825, a viscount in 1842 and died on 10 December of that year.

William Beresford

Beresford was born on 2 October 1768, the illegitimate son of the Earl of Tyrone, later the first Marquess of Waterford, a nobleman from whom he was never to lack patronage. He was sent to the military school at Strasbourg and in August 1785 was given an ensigncy in the 6th Foot. By 1793 he was captain in the 69th, then serving as marines aboard the Mediterranean fleet, and, after the siege of Toulon, he first attracted attention during operations in Corsica, for which he was granted a brevet-majority. He was promoted lieutenant-

Sir William Beresford, later Viscount Beresford, in the uniform of a marshal of the Portuguese army. After Lawrence. (National Army Museum)

colonel in August 1794, taking the 88th Foot to India in 1799 and commanding it during the Egyptian expedition. As a brigade commander he took part in the recapture of the Cape of Good Hope in 1806, and later the same year took Buenos Aires with only two battalions. However, he was not reinforced and, following a mass uprising, he was compelled to surrender after some hard fighting. Whitelocke's expedition failed to relieve him and Beresford remained in prison for six months, until he escaped and returned to England. At the end of 1807 he was sent to occupy Madeira, where he learned Portuguese, which was to stand him in good stead later on.

He was promoted major-general in April 1808 and, after fighting in the Corunna campaign, was given the task of reorganizing the Portuguese Army with the rank of marshal and local lieutenant-general in the British army in Portugal, a step which placed him above several more senior officers. With the aid of a few British officers, he set about converting what was little more than an unwieldy, chaotic rabble into a small disciplined force. Many of the existing officers he sacked as worthless, replacing them by younger men of ability, rather than position; the conscription laws were rigidly enforced, deserters were shot, and the best material was all grouped into the regiments singled out for the field army, while the remainder was formed into a militia. Picked men were chosen to form the *Caçador* battalions. Infringements of the stern discipline he imposed were ruthlessly punished but good conduct was suitably rewarded. Many of his measures earned him enormous unpopularity in Portugal, but within a year the effectiveness of his endeavours began to be demonstrated by the performance of Portuguese regiments at Busaco.

He held no field command with the Portuguese Army, his task being organization, administration and training, and in any case, although some Portuguese divisions were formed, Wellington was convinced that they were best employed in separate brigades incorporated into British divisions. Beresford's first big command in the field, that of Hill's corps during the latter's absence in England, was an unhappy experience and resulted in the bloody and ill-fought Battle of Albuera in 1811, where his inept handling of his force was redeemed by the gallantry of the British infantry. Thereafter he returned to his work with the Portuguese and, though he was present with the main army in the 1812 campaign and was wounded at Salamanca, he held no command and merely exercised a general supervision over the Portuguese troops.

After continuing in much the same capacity during the Battles of Vittoria and the Pyrenees, he was given the occasional command of a corps during the fighting in southern France, but always under Wellington's close watch. Following the Battle of Orthes, he was sent with a force of just over two divisions to support a royalist uprising in Bordeaux, but as no opposition was encountered,

Sir Denis Pack (1772–1823) in the embroidered uniform of a major-general, with lapels buttoned back. Commanded 71st Foot at Rolica and Vimiero, 1808, and a Portuguese brigade from 1810–13. Major-General, 1813. Commanded a British brigade in the 6th Division from 1813–14 and the Division itself at Sorauren. Eight wounds in the Peninsula. At Waterloo in command of a brigade in the 5th Division and again wounded. (National Army Museum)

Wellington and staff officers at the Battle of Fuentes d'Onoro, 1811. Note the party of light infantry escorting two French officer prisoners into headquarters. After Major St Clair (detail). (National Army Museum)

his competence was not greatly tested. At Toulouse Wellington ordered him to turn the French flank with the 4th and 6th Divisions, a task he completed with energy and efficiency.

Beresford was a man of great height and strength—his one-armed feat of unhorsing the Polish lancer at Albuera is famous—and his discoloured left eye, injured in a shooting accident, gave him a somewhat disconcerting appearance. Despite his failure in independent command, Wellington seems to have thought highly of him, saying he was the man with 'the largest view' among general officers, and that since only Beresford would know how to feed an army, he was Wellington's most suitable successor.

After the Peninsular War he was made a baron and returned to Portugal, where he stayed until he left for England in 1822 to go into politics. He became a viscount in 1823, a general in 1825 and served in Wellington's first cabinet in 1828. He died on 8 January 1854.

Thomas Picton

Born in 1758, the son of a Welsh country gentleman, Picton received an ensigncy in the 12th Foot at the age of thirteen. After reaching the rank of captain seven years later, he was placed on half-pay for the next twelve years and spent his time in Pembrokeshire studying his profession. In 1794, still without employment, he sailed on his own initiative for the West Indies where he was taken on the staff of the general in command. He stayed there until 1803, proving his ability as a soldier and reaching the rank of lieutenant-colonel, but his robust and vigorous rule as Governor of Trinidad brought him to trial on charges of cruelty in 1806. He was found guilty but was cleared at a second trial.

In 1808 he was promoted major-general and two years later was appointed to the 3rd Division in Portugal. He commanded this division throughout the Peninsular War except for a short break when wounded, showing himself to be a stern disciplinarian and a courageous, determined and farsighted commander. Too cold and blunt ever to be loved like Hill, he was always respected and made the 3rd Division one of the finest fighting formations in the army.

His first major action was Busaco in 1810, when his strong, tough personality and speed of decision defeated a major French attack. When Wellington advanced from the Lines of Torres Vedras in 1811 in pursuit of Massena, Picton's division played an important part in the operations, culminating in the Battle of Fuentes d'Onoro. In September Picton again displayed his skill and coolness in action when his division was attacked on the march at El Bodon by fifteen squadrons of cavalry, supported by horse artillery. Rather than halt the whole division and form square, he continued the march, protecting his flanks and rear by a series of leap-frogging battalion squares.

He was made a local lieutenant-general at this time, a rank which was confirmed in June 1813. In January 1812 he led the 3rd Division to the assault of Ciudad Rodrigo, storming the main breach, while the Light Division attacked the other. Wellington wrote: 'The conduct of the 3rd Division in the operations which they performed with so much gallantry affords the strongest proof of the abilities of Lt-Gen Picton'. Two months later, at the fierce and bloody siege of Badajoz, Picton personally led the storming of the castle. Though wounded and lying disabled in a ditch, he continued to urge his men on with his great voice until victory was theirs.

He was invalided home, created a Knight of the Bath in February 1813, and returned to Spain in time for the great victory at Vittoria. Impatient with waiting for the 7th Division, with whom he was to advance, he led the 3rd to a surprise attack on the French right flank, roaring at his men: 'Come on ye damned rascals, come on ye fighting villains!' Though he suffered nearly 2,000 casualties, he caused the collapse of the French right. On over the Pyrenees and into France he led his fighting division until the Battle of Toulouse concluded the campaign.

When the peerages were awarded after the war, for Picton, who was only a divisional commander, there was none, only the G.C.B. He said: 'If the coronet was lying at the crown of a breach, I should have as good a chance as any of them'. Neverthe-

Sir Thomas Picton in the pre-1812 uniform of a lieutenant-general with the lapels buttoned across and wearing the Star of the Order of the Bath, awarded in 1813. After Shee. (National Army Museum)

Picton's round hat and spurs. (National Army Museum)

stopped the French infantry dead, and ordered them forward in the counter-attack, shouting: 'Charge! Hurrah! Hurrah!' A bullet struck him in the head and tumbled him dead from his saddle.

Galbraith Lowry Cole

Cole was born in Dublin on 1 May 1772, the second son of the first Earl of Enniskillen. He obtained a cornetcy in the 12th Light Dragoons in 1787, subsequently serving with various regiments and as ADC to Sir Charles Grey in the West Indies campaign of 1794, until he reached the rank of lieutenant-colonel in November of that year. He went through the Egyptian campaign as Military Secretary to Sir John Hely-Hutchinson, was made colonel in 1801, and in 1805 took command of the 27th Foot at Malta. He led this regiment in the Italian campaign of 1806, in which he was appointed to a brigade consisting of his own regiment and a composite battalion of grenadier companies, and acted as second-in-command to Sir John Stuart at the Battle of Maida.

Promoted major-general in 1808, he joined the Peninsular army the following year as commander of the 4th Division. At Busaco his division saw little action, but after Massena's withdrawal from before Torres Vedras, the 2nd and 4th Divisions were despatched under Beresford to besiege Badajoz. Hearing of Soult's approach, Beresford advanced to meet him, leaving Cole to cover his rear and destroy the accumulated siege material. Soult attacked Beresford at Albuera on 16 May 1811, Cole meanwhile having made a forced march by night to reach Albuera on the morning of the attack. At the critical moment of the battle, Cole, who had been in reserve, advanced on his own initiative to relieve Hoghton's hard-pressed brigade by attacking the French left. With his three Fusilier battalions and five Portuguese, he launched the famous and decisive counter-stroke which, though attacked by cavalry and infantry supported by artillery, swept the French from the field, but at heavy cost, Cole himself being among the wounded.

After going home in late 1811 to take his seat in the Commons as M.P. for Fermanagh, he rejoined

Major-General of Infantry, c. 1812. Note the aiguillette which replaced the epaulettes in late 1811. Brigade-major in undress uniform in background. After Hamilton Smith. (National Army Museum)

less, when Wellington summoned him for the Waterloo campaign, he came, though he had a presentiment it would be his last. Now aged fifty-six and in command of the 5th Division, he fought the long and desperate day at Quatre Bras, defending the vital cross-roads against infantry and cavalry attacks. Though badly wounded in the ribs, he remained in command, holding his men together by dint of his powerful personality. He concealed his wound from all but his servant, who bound him up, and though in considerable pain the next day, he took up position with his division in the centre of the line near La Haye Sainte. When D'Erlon's corps attacked that sector, Picton kept his men out of sight below the ridge until the division opposing him was only forty yards away. Then he brought his men to their feet, fired a massive volley which

Sir Galbraith Lowry Cole in the uniform of a lieutenant-general, c. 1814. The badge round his neck and the lower star on the left breast are of the Portuguese Order of the Tower and Sword; the upper star is the Bath. The cross and ribbon is the Army Gold Cross awarded for service at four battles with clasps for further battles. After Lawrence. (National Army Museum)

facing vastly superior numbers at Roncesvalles in the Pyrenees. Like many of the divisional commanders, Cole found himself at a loss without Wellington's supervision and, though he fought a hard delaying action, he decided to withdraw to Sorauren, despite orders to the contrary. However, Wellington's arrival restored the situation and Cole redeemed himself in the following two days' fighting, in which two of his battalions, his old 27th and the 48th, made a magnificent counter-attack against four French battalions.

At the Battle of Nivelle the 4th Division carried the important fortified village of Sare, and at Orthes Cole attacked the village of St Boes, the key to the French position. A month later, at Toulouse, when the sudden flight of a Spanish division left a dangerous gap, the 4th and 6th Divisions stormed the commanding height of Calvinet, thus restoring the position.

If lacking the ability for an independent command, Cole was a popular and competent divisional commander, who was noted for his good nature and kindness to all ranks. Wellington, whose hospitality was always a little spartan, observed that the best dinners were to be had at Cole's headquarters.

In 1815 Wellington asked for him as a divisional commander, but, having only just married, Cole said he would join as soon as his honeymoon was over. However, Waterloo was fought before he could do so. He served with the army of occupation until 1818, and in later life, from 1828–33, was a popular and successful Governor of the Cape. He died on 4 October 1842.

Robert Craufurd

Born on 5 May 1764, the third son of a Scottish baronet, Craufurd received his first commission in 1779 as ensign in the 25th Foot. From 1783, as a captain on half-pay, he spent four years on the Continent studying the Prussian and other European armies. In 1787 he returned to England and transferred to the 75th Foot, a regiment newly raised for service in India against Tippoo Sahib. His superiors in the regiment being absent, the task of preparing it for war fell almost entirely on Craufurd as the senior captain, and he continued to

the army in time for Salamanca. The 4th Division was in the centre of the British line facing the French-held hills, the Arapiles. Supported on the left by Pack's Portuguese brigade, Cole attacked two French divisions, but, when Pack was thrown back, Cole's seven battalions became greatly outnumbered and outgunned. He had to retreat, but a crucial situation was saved by the 6th Division blocking the French counter-attack. Cole was again wounded but was able to rejoin his division in time to cover the retreat from Burgos.

In March 1813 he was invested with the Order of the Bath and in June promoted lieutenant-general. He continued in command of the 4th Division during the Vittoria campaign, and in July found himself detached from Wellington's command and

Robert Craufurd in the embroidered uniform of a major-general, c. 1812. (National Army Museum)

command it in the campaign against Tippoo, which lasted until 1792. He proved himself a stern disciplinarian and a most able commander in the field, but despite this and representations made by his brother on his behalf, the authorities were unwilling to grant him a majority. In 1793 he therefore resigned his commission, a step which lost him considerable seniority later. As a civilian, he joined his brother, who was British liaison officer with the Austrians in the Netherlands in 1793, thereafter obtaining commissions in two foreign regiments, Waldstein's and Hompesch's (later in British pay), between 1795 and 1797. He acted as British Military Attaché with the Austrians in Italy, subsequently being gazetted lieutenant-colonel in the 60th. After serving on the staff in the Irish Rebellion of 1798 and in Holland in 1799, he was sent to Switzerland to raise troops for British service. His study of his profession and his experience of foreign troops made him one of the best qualified officers in the army, but his advancement was slow, due, perhaps, to his violent temper.

In 1807, now a full colonel, he commanded a brigade of light troops during Whitelocke's hopeless expedition to Buenos Aires, and though compelled to surrender through no fault of his own, he established a reputation as a leader of light infantry. In late 1808 he joined Sir John Moore's army as commander of the brigade trained by Moore himself at Shorncliffe, the 43rd and 52nd Light Infantry and 95th Rifles. With this force Craufurd protected the rear of Moore's army during the initial stages of the retreat to Corunna. A rifleman wrote: 'General Craufurd was indeed one of the few men who was apparently created for command during such dreadful scenes as we were familiar with in this retreat. He seemed an iron man; nothing daunted him, nothing turned him from his purpose'.

Craufurd and his light brigade returned to the Peninsula later in 1809, joining the army just after Talavera, having made his celebrated forced march of forty-two miles in twenty-six hours. The brigade was immediately pushed forward on outpost duty and covered the subsequent retreat of the army to Portugal. Early in 1810 the Light Brigade was expanded into a division by the addition of two Portuguese *caçador* battalions and Craufurd, though still only a comparatively junior brigadier-general, was placed in command of it.

His finest achievement with the Light Division was his guarding of the forty-mile stretch of the River Agueda in north-east Portugal during the first five months of 1810, against a force six times his strength. His line was never pierced, his troops were never surprised, and the French were denied any intelligence of what was going on in Craufurd's rear. Sadly he marred this splendid record by choosing to engage Ney's entire corps on the wrong side of the River Coa in July 1810, thus disobeying his orders and risking his division. Nevertheless he held the bridge across the Coa and extricated his division with minimum loss.

He showed his best talents again at Busaco by a masterly delaying action against Ney's corps, followed by a decisive counter-stroke at precisely the right moment. He went home on leave in the winter of 1810, returning for Fuentes d'Onoro in May 1811, when the Light Division was sent out to rescue and cover the retreat of the almost sur-

Major-General Hill

RICHARD HOOK

A

Brigadier-General Craufurd

B

RICHARD HOOK

Major-General Picton

RICHARD HOOK

C

Major-General Lowry Cole

D

RICHARD HOOK

Lieutenant-General Beresford

RICHARD HOOK

E

Lieutenant-General Stapleton Cotton

General The Earl of Wellington

RICHARD HOOK

G

Lieutenant-General The Earl of Uxbridge

rounded 7th Division. Craufurd carried out the task with great skill, and then withdrew his own men across two miles of open ground under constant attack by French cavalry with the loss of only fifty men. He was promoted major-general in June 1811. On 24 January 1812 the Light Division suffered a great loss when their commander died of his wounds received during the assault on the breach at Ciudad Rodrigo. A short, dark man with flashing eyes and fiery disposition, Craufurd made many enemies, never suffering fools gladly; but he also had his admirers, particularly among the rank and file, and he was, without doubt, one of Wellington's most brilliant officers.

Charles von Alten

Of a number of Hanoverians who achieved general officer's rank in Wellington's armies, probably the best known—and the only one to command a British, as opposed to a King's German Legion, formation—was Charles von Alten. A member of an ancient Protestant family, he was born on 12 October 1764, the youngest son of Baron Alten. Appointed to a commission in the Hanoverian Foot Guards in 1781, he fought in the Hanoverian service during the Duke of York's campaign in the Low Countries between 1793 and 1795. Here he made a name as a commander of light troops when in charge of a line of outposts along the River Lys.

After Napoleon's conquest of Hanover in 1803, its army was disbanded, but the officers and men were permitted to go where they chose. Many went to England to form the King's German Legion, a force of all arms which, in January 1805, included two light battalions. Command of these was given to Alten, who led them during Lord Cathcart's expedition to Hanover in November, and in the Copenhagen operations of 1807. He accompanied Sir John Moore to Sweden in 1808 and later to Spain, where his battalions formed the 2nd Flank Brigade of Paget's Reserve. He served at Walcheren in 1809 and, after being promoted major-general on 25 July 1810, returned to the Peninsula, where he commanded an independent K.G.L. brigade at Albuera. This brigade subsequently joined the newly formed 7th Division, which was commanded by Alten from October 1811.

Sir Charles von Alten, later Count von Alten, as a major-general, c. 1813. After Heaphy. (National Portrait Gallery)

After Craufurd was killed at Ciudad Rodrigo in 1812, the Light Division was temporarily under Barnard, one of its brigadiers, and then Vandeleur, but on 2 May this important and élite formation was given to Alten, who was to command it until the end of the Peninsular War. Though lacking Craufurd's brilliance, he was a competent and conscientious officer who, unlike Craufurd, could be relied upon to obey Wellington's orders implicitly. Under him the Light Division maintained the very high standard it had achieved previously, both in the performance of outpost duties and on the field of battle. It led the advance to Salamanca in mid-1812, and in 1813, with the 4th Division, it formed the right centre of the British attack at Vittoria, quickly carrying its objectives. In these operations Alten was working under Wellington's eye, but during the battles in the Pyrenees he was on his own and, despite a great feat of marching and counter-marching for nineteen consecutive hours over mountain tracks, culminating in a brisk engagement, he just failed to cut off Soult's retreat from Sorauren at the Yanci bridge. At the Battle of Vera on 7 October 1813, fought in support of the crossing of the Bidassoa, Alten led his division in a very rapid attack up the Great Rhune. A month later, at the Nivelle, he made another fine attack on the Lesser Rhune, rolling up the French defences from a flank of this very rugged feature. At the Nive, he was attacked by four French divisions, but made an orderly retreat to a stronger position in rear, where he held firm. Wellington thought the Light Division under Alten was 'the flower of the army, the finest infantry in the world', and when the Peninsular army broke up, Alten was presented with a sword of honour subscribed for by the officers of the division as a mark of their respect. He was made a K.C.B. on 2 January 1815.

In the Waterloo campaign Alten was given the 3rd Division of three brigades, one British (C. Halkett), one K.G.L. (Ompteda), and one Han-

overian (Kielmansegge). After fighting at Quatre Bras, his division was placed in the right centre of Wellington's line, just behind La Haye Sainte. Though he held this position throughout the day, he made one bad mistake by ordering two of Ompteda's battalions to counter-attack in line in the presence of French cavalry, just after the loss of La Haye Sainte. They were badly cut up, and Alten himself was severely wounded and had to leave the field.

He was made a count after Waterloo and, when the K.G.L. was disbanded in 1816, was given command of the Hanoverian contingent of the Allied army of occupation in Paris. In 1818 he returned to Hanover as Minister of War and

Wellington and ADCs in the Pyrenees, 1813. The soldier behind the horse possibly represents his orderly, Corporal Baeckefeld, 1st Hussars, King's German Legion. After Atkinson. (National Army Museum)

Foreign Affairs, and Inspector-General of the Hanoverian Army, in which he became a field-marshal. He was made a G.C.B. on 12 August 1820 and died in the Tyrol on 20 April 1840.

Edward Pakenham

Born in 1778, the second son of Baron Longford, Pakenham entered the army at the age of sixteen. He served as a major in the 23rd Light Dragoons in the Irish Rebellion of 1798, obtaining the lieutenant-colonelcy of the 64th Foot a year later and serving with that regiment in campaigns in the West Indies from 1801–03. He exchanged to the 7th Royal Fusiliers in 1805, and commanded its first battalion at Copenhagen in 1807 and in Martinique in 1809. Later that year he joined the Peninsular army as a staff officer, soon becoming Deputy-Adjutant-General at Wellington's headquarters.

At Busaco he commanded a brigade of the 1st Division, later transferring to the 4th Division but retaining his brigade until January 1811. He then reverted to the staff but took over the brigade again later in the year. He was made a local major-general in 1811 and received that rank in the army a year after.

When Picton was wounded at Badajoz, Pakenham took over the 3rd Division. At Salamanca he was ordered by Wellington to attack the leading division of Marmont's army, while the other divisions attacked the French in flank. This Pakenham did brilliantly, completely routing Thomières' division and pressing on to drive back the next. After the battle Wellington wrote of him: 'He made the movement with a celerity and accuracy which I doubt if there are very many capable, and without both it would not have answered its end. Pakenham may not be the brightest genius but my partiality for him does not lead me astray when I tell you that he is one of the best we have'.

Pakenham remained in command of the 3rd Division until the end of the year, and early in 1813 was given the 6th Division. He was appointed Wellington's Adjutant-General in June, but had to take over the 6th again in the closing stages of the Battle of Sorauren, when its temporary commander, Pack, was wounded. In the final attack on 30 July Pakenham led his division in the assault on the village of Sorauren itself and, notwithstanding its heavy fortifications, he inflicted heavy losses on the French division opposing him, which ceased to exist as an effective force. In September he was made a Knight of the Bath. He returned to his post of Adjutant-General in August and continued in that capacity until the end of the Peninsular War.

Pakenham himself disliked staff work, referring to it as 'this insignificant clerking business', and much preferred being in command of troops. Nevertheless he performed the duties of Adjutant-General effectively and to Wellington's great satisfaction. He enjoyed a good and close relationship with his chief, being not only devoted to him but also his brother-in-law.

In the closing stages of the war with America (1812–15) Pakenham was appointed to the command, after his predecessor, Ross, was killed at Bladensburg. Arriving in December 1814, he found his troops had been landed in a most unsatisfactory position before New Orleans. Unable to rectify this deployment, he ordered an unimaginative assault for 8 January 1815. It was beaten back with disastrous loss and Pakenham himself was killed. Four days before his death he had been made a G.C.B.

George Murray

Murray differed from the other generals in this book in that the whole of his service under Wellington's command was spent on the staff, rather than in command of troops. He became Wellington's most trusted staff officer and developed a very close working relationship with his chief.

He was born in 1772, the second son of a Scottish baronet, Sir William Murray of Ochtertyre, and was educated at the High School and University of Edinburgh. His military career started as an ensign in the 71st Foot in 1789, transferring to the 3rd Foot

Guards in 1790. He served with his regiment in Flanders from 1793–95 and received his first staff appointment in 1796 as ADC to Major-General Campbell in the expedition to Quiberon Bay. He was on the Quartermaster-General's staff in the Netherlands in 1799 and was wounded. After going through the Egyptian campaign in the same capacity, he attended a course of study at the Senior Department at the Royal Military College at High Wycombe, and afterwards went as Adjutant-General to the West Indies. He returned to the Quartermaster-General's department for the expeditions to Hanover and Copenhagen. In 1808 he was appointed Quartermaster-General to Moore's Swedish expedition and subsequently accompanied Moore in the Corunna campaign.

In March 1809, by now a brevet-colonel, he became Wellington's Quartermaster-General in the Peninsula, a post he continued to hold, except for a gap in 1812, until the end of the war. He was promoted brigadier-general on 4 June 1811 and major-general on 1 January 1812.

Murray was ideally suited to this work. He was calm, methodical, well-mannered, with an excellent memory, an aptitude for history and geography, and had behind him staff experience in all the most important campaigns of the French wars. He was both quick and accurate in interpreting Wellington's wishes and transmitting his orders to the component parts of the army. Wellington exercised very close supervision over his army, much closer than many commanders, and though he trusted Murray completely and had him constantly in attendance, listening to his views and recommendations, he allowed him only limited powers of decision. Nevertheless, he relied on him greatly, and when, in 1812, Murray applied to go home for private reasons, Wellington wrote: 'I acknowledge that when I first heard of your intention to quit us, my sentiments were not confined to concern and regret.' After the Peninsular War, he pronounced Murray to be 'a very able man and an admirable Quartermaster-General'. One of the most valuable of Murray's many duties was his control of a network of agents and observing officers, who provided intelligence about the enemy and topography. For his work Murray was made a Knight of the Bath.

At the end of 1814 he was appointed to the staff of

Sir George Murray as a major-general, c. 1813. After Heaphy. (National Portrait Gallery)

the army in America with the local rank of lieutenant-general. When Napoleon escaped from Elba he was recalled to Europe, and though arriving too late for Waterloo, was subsequently Chief of Staff to the Allied army of occupation and Quartermaster-General of the British contingent, a post he held until 1818.

In later life he acted as Governor of the Royal Military College at Sandhurst (1819–24), Lieutenant-General of the Ordnance (1824), Commander-in-Chief in Ireland (1825–28), Colonial Secretary and a Privy Councillor (1828–30), and twice as Master-General of the Ordnance (1834–35 and 1841–46). He also served as M.P. for Perthshire. He became a general in 1841 and died in 1846.

The Plates

The Uniform of General and Staff Officers

The uniform for general officers according to the Clothing Regulations in force in 1802 was as follows. The black cocked hat, increasingly worn fore-and-aft instead of athwart, had a black cockade and a gilt scale loop with button, surmounted by a white feather with red at the base. At each corner were crimson and gold tassels. Their scarlet coats had blue patches at either end of the collar, small indented blue cuffs, and blue lapels down to the waist which could either be buttoned back to show the blue and fastened in front with hooks and eyes or buttoned across the body making the coat double-breasted. The long skirts were lined with white cassimere and hooked back, being fastened at the bottom with a gold-embroidered scarlet ornament. There was a gilt button on the blue collar patches, nine or ten down each lapel, three or four set vertically on each skirt and cuff, and two at the back at hip level. Generals had their buttons at equal distances, lieutenant-generals in threes, major-generals and brigadier-generals in pairs, except the latter had their skirt and cuff buttons set two over one. On each shoulder was worn an epaulette of gold embroidery on scarlet cloth with gold bullion fringe. There were two types of coat: the embroidered version, which had gold-embroidered loops on all the buttonholes, including the collar, cuffs and skirts, and the plain or undress coat which was without embroidery, but normally had the buttonholes marked by loops of narrow twist the same colour as the cloth.

White cloth or cassimere breeches with black-topped boots were to be worn with either coat, and the dress was completed by a crimson sash worn round the waist with the knot and ends at the left side. The sword was suspended by a white waist belt with slings and fastened by a snake clasp between two lions' heads.

Following a General Order dated 24 December 1811, certain alterations were made which will be noted in the relevant plate notes.

Senior staff officers wore the same uniform as general officers but with silver lace. The uniform of Adjutant- and Quartermaster-Generals corresponded to that of a lieutenant-general, and Deputy AGs and QMGs to a major-general. Assistant and Deputy Assistant AGs and QMGs, Brigade-Majors and ADCs had single-breasted coats without lapels and with all-blue collars, ADCs having gold lace embroidery, the others silver.

In the field, following the example of Wellington himself, the dress of generals and staff officers often diverged from that prescribed by regulations, and some examples will be found in the individual plates.

(Readers requiring further details are directed to the *Journal of the Society for Army Historical Research*, Vol. XIX, p. 200, Vol. XXII, p. 339, Vol. XXXI, pp. 64 and 96.)

A Major-General Hill

This plate shows Hill at Talavera on the evening of 27 July 1809, just before the French made a surprise

General and field officers' Army Gold Medal for distinguished service, 1810–13. This example was awarded for an action in the East Indies. The ribbon was crimson, edged blue. (National Army Museum)

attack on the Cerro de Medellin hill, held by his division, when, in his own words, he 'was with the 48th Regiment in conversation with Colonel Donellan'. It also illustrates his never-failing kindness to ordinary soldiers, in this case Donellan's orderly drummer. Hill's 2nd Division contained two battalions of the 48th, which played a prominent part in the battle, and Donellan's counter-attack on the 28th earned Wellington's commendation that 'the battle was certainly saved by the advance, position and steady conduct of the 48th Regiment'.

Hill wears the embroidered coat of a major-general with the lapels buttoned across except at the top, showing the gold embroidery on the buttonholes. Dark tight-fitting pantaloons and hessian boots are worn in preference to the regulation lower garments. According to the 1802 Regulations, generals were to have a straight sword of the 1796 infantry pattern, although another type with a gilt boat-shell, similar to the heavy cavalry officers' 1796 sword, was also used. In 1803 a new pattern with a lion's head pommel was introduced for general officers, but the former types continued to be carried, and many officers, particularly those like Hill who had served in Egypt, preferred the mameluke sabre.

Lieutenant-Colonel Donellan of the 1st/48th, though an efficient and much-loved commanding officer, indulged in certain eccentricities of appearance, which gave him the nickname of 'the last of the powderers'. Though the practice of powdering the hair had been abolished in 1795 and the queue discontinued in 1808, Donellan ignored both changes and was also well known for his habit of wearing the cocked hat, breeches and top boots in the fashion of the previous decade. In accordance with the regulations for regiments with buff facings, his breeches and sword belt are of that colour and, as a field officer, he wears epaulettes on both shoulders. The lapels of his coat are buttoned across. He was mortally wounded at Talavera while leading his battalion to the attack.

His orderly drummer wears a shako instead of the full dress bearskin cap and his jacket is in reversed colours as authorized for drummers. His breeches are covered by white overalls and he is armed with a short sword with a twenty-four-inch blade.

Sir William Ponsonby (1772–1815) in the uniform of a major-general. Commanded the 5th Dragoon Guards in the Peninsula from 1811–12 and took over Le Marchant's heavy brigade on the latter's death at Salamanca, commanding it until 1814. Major-general in 1813. In command of the Union Brigade of heavy cavalry at Waterloo and killed during the retreat after its charge. (National Army Museum)

B Brigadier-General Craufurd

Craufurd is represented here shortly after taking command of the newly formed Light Division in early 1810, discussing outpost positions along the River Agueda with officers of the 95th Rifles and Ross's Troop, Royal Horse Artillery. The Rifles performed for the Light Division what the Division performed for the Peninsular army and were highly skilled at outpost duties, earning a special commendation from Craufurd, who was never lavish with praise, for their night action at the bridge of Barba del Puerco in March 1810. Ross's Troop was the only horse artillery attached to an infantry division and, with the 1st Hussars, King's German Legion, gave invaluable support to Craufurd's 'Light Bobs'.

Craufurd wears the plain or undress coat of a brigadier-general, as he then was, with overalls. He is armed with the 1803-pattern sword, suspended from an undress waist belt of black leather.

The Rifleman is based on a contemporary drawing made by an officer of the regiment in the Peninsula and shows the light cavalry style affected by its officers. Although the rifle-green jacket had three rows of silver buttons, the pelisse, which is, rather curiously, half worn and half slung, had black olivets instead of buttons. The jacket is faced black and the pelisse trimmed with brown fur. His grey overalls are reinforced with brown leather in a decorative fashion and have black braid down the outside seams. His shako is similar to the watering caps worn by cavalry officers, tapering towards the top and with a folding peak. A whistle is attached to the silver lion's head fitted to the black leather pouch belt. The sabre is also of light cavalry pattern.

The R.H.A. officer's dress also emulates the light cavalry, including the light dragoon helmet of black leather with fur crest, and, except for the colours, is very similar to the 95th officer's dress.

33

Wellington and staff at Waterloo. Uxbridge can be seen galloping towards Wellington and the dying figure in the right centre foreground is probably Picton. The mounted figure on the grey behind may be Hill. After Atkinson. (National Army Museum)

C Major-General Picton

The incident depicted in this plate occurred at Busaco in 1810, when, according to Oman, 'the light companies of the 45th and 88th . . . were rallied by Picton in person, and brought up along the plateau to the right of the 8th Portuguese'.

Picton was notorious for his indifference to regulation dress and his example was followed by his staff, resulting in their being known in the Peninsular army as 'the bear and ragged staff', an allusion to the arms of the Earl of Warwick. He usually wore a blue military frock coat or a civilian coat. At Vittoria he was seen in a broad-brimmed beaver hat to protect his eyes and in the Waterloo campaign he appeared entirely in civilian clothes. He usually carried a stick or an umbrella. However, his great frame and bellowing voice, 'with the power of twenty trumpets', was so well known in the army that he needed none of the trappings of a general officer to distinguish himself. When the French attacked up the Busaco ridge at dawn,

Picton sprang straight from his bed into action, forgetting to remove his red night cap, in which he is shown here, and doubtless putting on the first coat that came to hand.

The Light Company soldier of the 88th Connaught Rangers recalls the long-standing feud between Picton and that regiment, which served in his division throughout the war. Though he admired the 88th's great fighting qualities, he deplored their indiscipline out of action. The soldier wears the felt, 1805 version of the 'stovepipe' shako, originally introduced in 1800, with the green tuft of the light infantry companies. His red jacket has the wings of a flank company. Trousers, usually white, grey or blue were taken into regular use during the Peninsular War, often being worn over the regulation white breeches. He is accoutred with his pouch, knapsack with greatcoat rolled on top, haversack and water bottle.

The third figure is an officer of the 8th Portuguese Regiment of the Line, whose conduct at Busaco proved the increasing effectiveness of Beresford's reforms of the Portuguese army. Although officially in Leith's 5th Division, the regiment served under Picton's command at

Busaco. He wears the 1806 uniform with the blue collar and yellow cuffs, piped red, of the 8th. He is shown in the 1806-pattern shako, but this was being replaced from 1810 by a 'stove-pipe' shape, resembling the British infantry headdress. The brass plate bears the arms of the House of Braganza, a motif that is repeated on the gorget and shoulder belt plate. He wears a captain's epaulettes, consisting of shoulder straps covered in metal scales and terminating in short fringes.

D Major-General Lowry Cole

George Napier of the 52nd said of Lowry Cole, commanding the 4th Division, 'he is as kind and generous as he is brave'. This plate represents an incident during the retreat to Torres Vedras after Busaco, when Cole gave shelter and rest to the wounded Napier, an officer of another division, who had been abandoned by the Portuguese driver of the cart in which he had been travelling.

Cole is dressed as he might have been for dinner at his headquarters, wearing his major-general's embroidered coat with the lapels buttoned back and unhooked to show the white waistcoat, dark blue pantaloons and hessian boots.

Napier wears the scarlet jacket with buff facings, silver lace and buttons in pairs of the 52nd Light Infantry, serving in the Light Division. His grey overalls are reinforced round the bottom with leather. Light infantry officers carried sabres instead of the straight infantry sword, and wore them suspended from a shoulder belt with slings instead of the more usual frog.

The sentry at Cole's door is from one of the regiments of his division, the 7th Royal Fusiliers. In action fusilier regiments wore the shako like other Line regiments, but here he is wearing his full dress bearskin cap, and to further smarten himself up for this duty has removed his trousers to reveal the regulation white breeches and black gaiters. It was two battalions of this regiment and one of the 23rd

Front and rear views of a major-general's embroidered coat, post-1811, with aiguillette. The latter was looped up to the buttons on the right lapel. (National Army Museum)

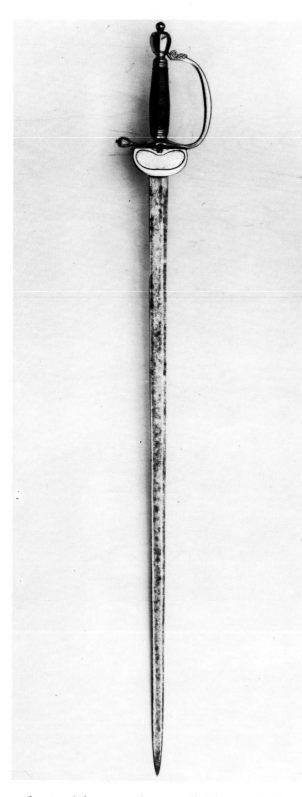

1796-pattern infantry sword, as prescribed for general officers by the 1802 regulations. The guard was brass and the grip bound with silver wire. The sword knot was crimson and gold and the scabbard black leather with gilt mounts. (National Army Museum)

Royal Welch Fusiliers that formed Myers' Fusilier brigade of Cole's division, which delivered the decisive counter-stroke at Albuera.

E Lieutenant-General Beresford

Though Beresford's chief role in the Peninsula was the reorganization of the Portuguese army, he fought at Albuera in 1811 as a lieutenant-general in the British army while temporarily in command of Hill's corps. During the height of the battle he personally tried to bring forward Carlos de España's Spanish brigade to support Hoghton's hard-pressed British brigade (29th, 48th, and 57th). Although some Spanish formations fought well at Albuera, this was not one of them, and they refused to advance, despite Beresford dragging forward one of the Spanish colonels by his epaulettes—the incident depicted here.

Beresford is wearing the cocked hat of a British general but with the red and blue cockade of Portugal added to the black British one. As shown in a contemporary print, he is dressed in a pelisse-coat with black frogging, strictly speaking an unofficial undress of light cavalry officers, but also popular with senior and staff officers. His sash and sword belt are of regulation British pattern.

The ADC helping Beresford to rally the Spaniards has an oilskin cover over his hat and, although on service blue frock coats were often worn by staff officers, he is shown here in the plain, single-breasted coat of his appointment in order to illustrate its details. Being an undress garment it lacks the tasselled, foliate gold lace loops (silver for brigade-majors) worn on the embroidered coat, and has the buttons in pairs down the front and set two over one on the cuffs and skirts. The single epaulette of gold (or silver) embroidery on blue cloth was worn on the right shoulder by infantry ADCs and brigade-majors, and on the left by those attached to cavalry commanders. Brigade-majors retained silver embroidery on the collar and cuffs of their undress coats. The ADC shown here wears a regulation staff sword belt and the 1796-pattern infantry sword.

Carlos de España's brigade included the regiments 'Rey', 'Zamora' and 'Volontarios de Navarra' and had been severely handled by the French earlier in the year. The Spanish field officer in the plate wears the white uniform with violet facings of the first-named regiment. This was the 1805 uniform which, by 1811, was soon to be replaced by a more practical dress, predominantly blue in colour. His cocked hat bears the red cockade of Spain.

F Lieutenant-General Stapleton Cotton
On 11 April 1812 Cotton, in command of the Cavalry Division, conducted a masterly action at Llerena against Soult's rearguard corps with W. Ponsonby's light cavalry brigade (12th, 14th, and 16th Light Dragoons) and Le Marchant's heavy brigade (5th Dragoon Guards, 3rd and 4th Dragoons). The plate shows Cotton as he might have appeared on this occasion, with an orderly dragoon of the 4th, giving an order to an officer of the 14th Light Dragoons attached to his staff.

Cotton was famous for his splendid appearance and is wearing the magnificent scarlet uniform with blue facings of a general officer of hussars, in which he is shown in Heaphy's paintings. Here he wears dark blue overalls, but on more ceremonial occasions these were replaced by scarlet breeches and hessian boots, and a white over red plume was fitted to the busby.

At this time the dress of the heavy and light cavalry was being changed in accordance with the new regulations of 1811–12, but it was some time before regiments in the Peninsula were re-equipped. The officer of the 14th Light Dragoons wears the old uniform of crested helmet and laced jacket, and is based on a portrait of an officer of that regiment painted in 1812. The 14th did not receive the new clothing until 1813 and an officer noted that he was still wearing the old helmet as late as May 1814. A blue pelisse trimmed with black fur and black braiding was also worn sometimes by officers of the 14th, but is not shown here. Officially the regiment's facings were orange, but in practice were almost scarlet. In the field, grey overalls with the double orange stripe were worn instead of the full dress white buckskin breeches.

The 4th Dragoons received their new clothing, with the exception of the helmet with horse-hair mane, about two weeks after the action at Llerena, so it must have been almost the last occasion the old dress was worn in action by this regiment. The old heavy cavalry headdress was still officially the cocked hat worn athwart, but in the field felt

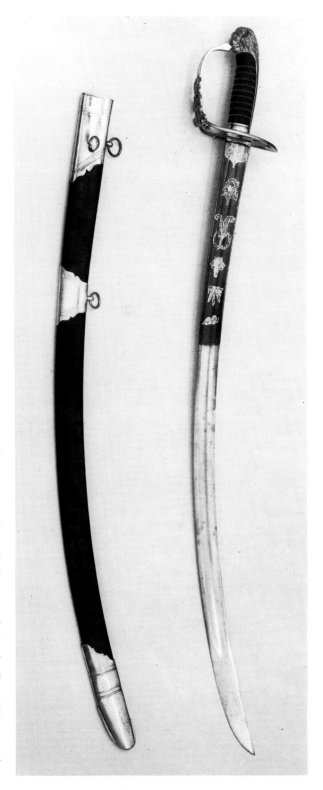

1803-pattern general officers' sword with scabbard. The guard and scabbard mounts were gilt brass and the grip was bound with brass wire. The Royal Cypher with crown above was inset in the guard. (National Army Museum)

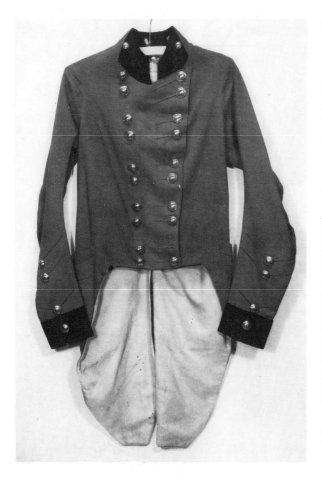
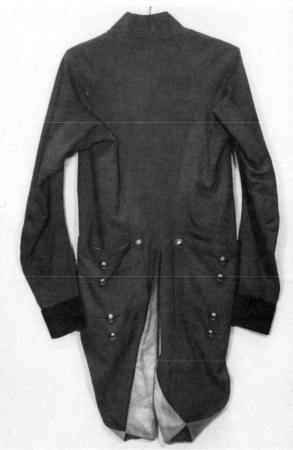

Front and rear views of a major-general's plain or undress coat. This example is buttoned across on the wrong side and the epaulettes or aiguillette are missing. (National Army Museum)

watering caps with a movable peak were more usually worn, as shown in the plate, and overalls replaced the white leather breeches and jacked boots. The dragoon is armed with the heavy cavalry 1796-pattern carbine and straight sword and, in addition to his pouch belt, carries a haversack and water bottle over the right shoulder.

G General The Earl of Wellington

The incident depicted in this plate shows Wellington, accompanied by his Military Secretary, Lord Fitzroy Somerset, ordering Major-General Pakenham, commanding the 3rd Division in Picton's absence, to attack the French left at the Battle of Salamanca, 22 July 1812. According to Lady Longford, *Wellington—The Years of the Sword*, the following exchange took place:

'Ned, d'ye see those fellows on the hill?',

Wellington said, tapping Pakenham on the shoulder, 'Throw your division into column; at them; and drive them to the devil'.

'I will, my lord, if you will give me your hand', replied Pakenham.

With his well-known campaigning costume of plain frock coat, white breeches and hessian boots, Wellington wears a low cocked hat, often encased in an oilskin cover, but here displaying the white ostrich feathers round the brim, as prescribed exclusively for general officers by General Order dated 24 December 1811. His sword belt and crimson sash are worn under his coat, as was his practice. Later in 1812, after being made *Generalissimo* of the Spanish forces, he took to wearing the red and gold sash of a Spanish general and added the cockades of Spain and Portugal to the black cockade of England in his hat. Under his coat he wears a white waistcoat and a white stock in preference to the more usual black. Sometimes his clothes might be grey and overalls would replace the breeches, but although he would don his general's, and later field-marshal's, scarlet coat for ceremonial occasions, his field dress always made a neat and restrained contrast to the showy attire of his opponents.

Pakenham wears the plain coat of a major-general. In accordance with the above-mentioned order of 1811, general's epaulettes were abolished in favour of an aiguillette worn on the right shoulder only; this was arranged differently according to the rank of the general officer. Besides adding the ostrich feathers to the hat, the 1811 order retained the scale loop for infantry generals but prescribed a star loop for those of the cavalry.

Somerset is dressed very similarly to his chief, except that his frock coat is double-breasted and he wears overalls reinforced with leather, a costume based on a description of Wellington's 'blue-coated staff' and a contemporary print by Atkinson of Wellington and staff at Salamanca. He carries a telescope in a leather case and a haversack covered in black oilskin to hold any writing materials, maps, etc., that his chief may require. Though only in his early twenties, Somerset served Wellington with devoted efficiency all through the Peninsular War and afterwards until Wellington's death in 1852, when as Lord Raglan he became Commander-in-Chief of the Army and held the chief command in the Crimea.

H Lieutenant-General The Earl of Uxbridge
This shows Lord Uxbridge, in command of the Allied cavalry during the Waterloo campaign, accompanied by an ADC from the 2nd Hussars, King's German Legion, giving orders to an officer of the 1st Life Guards, as they might have appeared at Genappe during the retreat from Quatre Bras.

The figure of Uxbridge is based on the Denis Dighton painting of Waterloo in the Royal Collection, which shows him in the uniform of a general officer of light cavalry. His shako, of the 1812 light dragoon pattern, bears a triple row of gold gimp, denoting his rank. He wears the fur-trimmed dark blue pelisse, with five rows of gilt buttons, over his jacket, though whether the latter was the scarlet pattern worn by general officers of hussars or the dark blue he was entitled to wear as colonel of the 7th Hussars is not known. Another painting by Dighton of the same incident shows him in light blue overalls cut in the cossack style,

but this cannot be correct as the actual overalls he wore, now in the possession of the Marquess of Anglesey, are dark blue. In full dress, general officers of hussars carried a mameluke sabre, but in the Waterloo campaign Uxbridge appears to have used the light cavalry pattern sabre with stirrup hilt.

Serving as an extra ADC was Captain von Streerwitz of the 2nd K.G.L. Hussars. The figure is shown in his regimental uniform with a forage cap covered in oilskin. In the plate he is wearing his pelisse slung, in order to show the details of the jacket, but in view of the weather on 17 June he would probably have been wearing it over the jacket, like Uxbridge.

The officer of the 1st Life Guards is dressed in

Embroidered coat of an ADC, c. 1815. Scarlet, faced blue, with gold lace. A brigade-major's coat was similar but with silver lace. The epaulette is missing. From late 1811 ADCs and brigade-majors attached to cavalry commanders wore an aiguillette instead of an epaulette, infantry staff keeping the latter. (National Army Museum)

accordance with the uniform changes of 1812. The black leather helmet with gilt fittings was surmounted by a crimson and blue silk 'chenille'. He wears the undress jacket, or frock collett, instead of the laced dress jacket, and cloth overalls. His belts and sabretache are all of the undress pattern. On service, officers of the Household Cavalry carried the ordinary heavy cavalry officer's sword as opposed to their more ornate parade sword with half-basket hilt.

(The author acknowledges with gratitude the help given by the Marquess of Anglesey in the preparation of this plate and by Mr John Mollo with this and other plates.)

Notes sur les planches en couleur

A Major-General Hill à la bataille de Talavera, le 27 juillet 1809. Il porte la tunique brodée d'un général de brigade avec les revers boutonnés sur la poitrine à l'exception de l'haut de revers; comme beaucoup d'officiers qui étaient au service en Egypte il porte un sabre mameluke en préférence à l'epée réglementaire. Avec lui sont un tambour du 48th Foot et Lieutenant-Colonel Donellan du même régiment qui continua à porter les cheveux en le style poudré démodé en dépit de consignes contres.

B Brigadier-General Craufurd visitant avant-postes de sa Division Légère au bord du fleuve Agueda en 1810. Il porte la tunique *undress* de ce grade. Avec lui sont un officier du 95th Regiment mis en la tenue verte typique des Chasseurs à Pied; et un officier du Royal Horse Artillery.

C Major-General Picton, un excentrique gallois grossier et intrépide, fut souvent vu en champ de bataille mis en vêtements civils. A Busaco en 1810 il fut réveillé de son lit à la bataille et il porta le bonnet de nuit rouge illustré. Il est illustré avec un soldat de la Compagnie Légère, 88th Foot, et un officier du 8eme Infanterie de Ligne de l'armée Portugaise, qui furent au service sous le commandement de lui avec distinction.

D Les mémoires de George Napier font mention de l'incident quand Napier, blessé, chercha l'abri chex le logement de Major-General Lowry Cole. Cette planche illustre Cole, mis en la tunique brodée de son grade, saluant à Napier, mis en la tenue d'un officier de la 52nd Light Infantry. Le sentinelle à la porte du général porte la grande tenue de la 7th Royal Fusiliers.

E A la bataille d'Albuera en 1811 Lieutenant-General Beresford essaya à amener la brigade espagnole de Carlos de España pour appuyer l'infanterie Brittanique aux abois mais il échoua à persuader les Espagnols d'attaquer quand même il tira un de leur colonels vers lui par ses épaulettes! Nous illustrons Beresford mis en une *pelisse-coat*, avec cocardes brittanique et portugaise dans son chapeau mis de coté. Le colonel est mis en la tenue du Régiment del Rey. Dans le fond est un aide de camp brittanique mis en tunique *undress*.

F Lieutenant-General Stapleton Cotton commandant la Division de Cavalerie à Llerena en avril 1812, mis en la tenue d'un général d'Hussars. Avec lui sont un planton de la 4th Dragoons et un officier de la 14th Light Dragoons.

G General The Earl of Wellington comme il fut en juillet 1812, à la bataille de Salamanca (Los Arapiles). Il est mis en civil de campagne ordinaire. Il est accompagné de son secretaire militaire Lord Fitzroy Somerset, et son beau-frère, Major-General Pakenham, commandant la 3rd Division. Pakenham porte la tunique ordinaire de son grade avec l'aiguilette que remplaça les épaulettes de grade de général en 1811. Somerset porte un costume similaire à son commandant en chef.

H Lieutenant-General The Earl of Uxbridge mis en la tenue d'un général de la Cavalerie Légère, ordonnant la retraite de l'armée alliée de Quatre Bras à Waterloo le 17 juin 1815. Avec lui est un aide, Captain von Streerwitz de la 2nd Hussars, King's German Legion, est un officier de la 1st Life Guards mis en tenue *undress*.

Farbtafeln

A Major-General Hill am 27 Juli 1809 an der Schlacht bei Talavera. Er trägt die bestickte Jacke eines Generalmajor mit den Aufschlägen über der Brust zugenknöpft bis auf den Oberteil; wie viele Offiziere, die in Ägypten dienten, trägt er einen mameluke Säbel lieber als ein Kommisssschwert. Mit ihm sind ein Trommler des 48th Foot, und Lieutenant-Colonel Donellan des gleichen Regiments, der die altmodische gepuderte Haarmode weiter trug trotz Befehlen dagegen.

B Brigadier-General Craufurd besichtigend in 1810 Vorposten seiner Leichtdivision an dem Agueda Fluss. Er trägt die *undress* Jacke dieses Dienstgrads. Mit ihm sin ein Offizier des 95ten Regiments in der typischen grünen Uniform der Schützenregimenter; und ein Offizier der Royal Horse Artillery.

C Major-General Picton, ein furchtloser walisischer exzentrischer Mensch, der ein loses Maul hatte, wurde oft in Zivilkleidern auf dem Schlachtfeld gesehen. In 1810 in Busaco wurde er aus seinem Bett zu der Schlacht aufgeboten und er trug die rote Schlafmütze, die hier illustriert wird. Er wird mit einem Soldat der Leichtkompagnie, 88th Foot, und einem Offizier der 8ten Linieninfanterie portugiesischer Armee, gesehen, die Dienst mit Auszeichnung unter seinem Befehl taten.

D Die Memoiren George Napiers erwähnen den Zwischenfall, als Napier, verwundet, Obdach bei dem Quartier Major-General Lowry Coles suchte. Diese Farbtafel illustriert Cole, in der bestickten Jacke seines Dienstgrads, grüssend an Napier in der Uniform eines Offiziers des 52nd Light Infantry. Der Posten an der Tür des Generals trägt die Galauniform des 7th Royal Fusiliers.

E In 1811 an der Schlacht bei Albuera versuchte Lieutenant-General Beresford die spanische Brigade Carlos de Españas anzuführen, um die hart bedrängte britische Infanterie zu unterstützen aber er verfehlte die Spaniers zu überfallen bereden, selbst, als er einen ihrer Obersten an seinen Epauletten herbeizog! Wir illustrieren Beresford in einer *pelisse-coat* mit britischen und portugiesischen Kokarden in seinem Hut. Der Oberst ist in der Uniform des Regiments del Rey. In dem Hintergrund ist ein britischer Adjutant in *undress* jacke.

F Lieutenant-General Stapleton Cotton in April 1812 in Befehl der Kavallereidivision in Llerena und er trägt die Uniform eines Generals Husars. Mit ihm sind ein Ordonanz des 4th Dragoons und ein Offizier des 14th Light Dragoons.

G General The Earl of Wellington, als er in Juli 1812 an der Schlacht bei Salamanca (Los Arapiles) war. Er trägt seinen gewöhnlichen Zivilfeldanzug. Er ist mit seinem Militärsekretar, Lord Fitzroy Somerset, und seinem Schwager, Major-General Pakenham, in Befehl der 3ten Division, begleitet. Pakenham trägt die ungemusterte Jacke seines Dienstgrads, mit der Achselschnur, die in 1811 die Epauletten Generalsdienstgrads ersassen. Somerset trägt ein gleiches Kostüm als das von seinem Oberbefehlshaber.

H Lieutenant-General The Earl of Uxbridge in der Uniform eines Generals Leichtkavallerie, am 17 Juni 1815 in Befehl von dem Rückzug der verbudeten Armee von Quatre-Bras nach Waterloo. Mit ihm ist ein Adjutant, Captain von Streerwitz des 2nd Hussars, King's German Legion; und ein Offizier des 1st Life Guards in *undress* uniform.